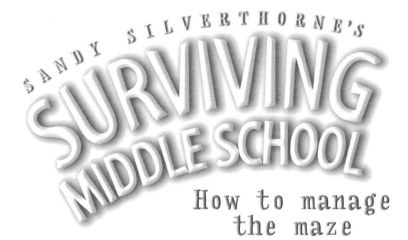

SANDY SILVERTHORNE'S

SURVIVING MIDDLE SCHOOL

How to manage the maze

Standard
PUBLISHING

CINCINNATI, OHIO

© 2003 Sandy Silverthorne. © 2003 Standard Publishing, Cincinnati, Ohio.
A division of Standex International Corporation. All rights reserved.
Printed in USA.
Project editor: Jennifer Holder. Cover and interior design: Robert Glover.
Typesetting: Peggy Theile

Scripture taken from the *New King James Version*. Copyright © 1982
by Thomas Nelson, Inc. Used by permission. All rights reserved.

Published in association with the literary agency of Alive Communications, Inc.,
7680 Goddard Street., Suite 200, Colorado Springs, Colorado, 80920.

ISBN 0-7847-1433-9

09 08 07 06 05 04   9 8 7 6 5 4 3 2

TABLE OF CONTENTS

MOVIN' ON UP

You're about to start middle school. Wow! New people! Different classes! Sports! Snack machines! Or if you're like a lot of kids, you may be thinking, "Yikes! Huge classes! Strange teachers! Big, impersonal buildings! Whose idea was this middle school thing anyway?"

Moving up to middle school is a change. And change can be hard. You're probably excited to do a new thing because you're growing up, but at the same time, a little nervous because you've never done this before.

Well, don't worry, this book is full of time-tested solutions for you not only to survive middle school, but to actually thrive there!

This book will help you discover the ins and outs of this new experience. So hang on, this is going to be fun!

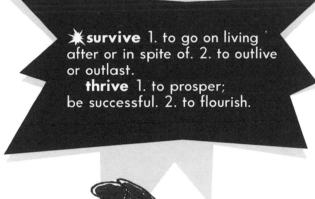

survive 1. to go on living after or in spite of. 2. to outlive or outlast.
    thrive 1. to prosper; be successful. 2. to flourish.

Doesn't thriving sound better?

As Kevin looked for his math class,
it hadn't occurred to him he had his
campus map upside down . . .

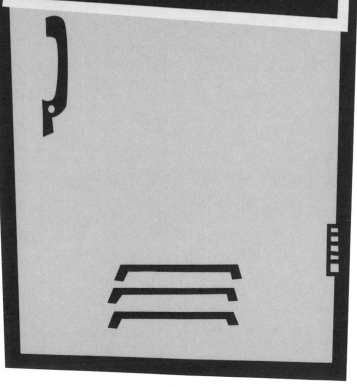

CHAPTER 1:

A day in the life of a middle schooler

This is the day which the Lord has made;
We will rejoice and be glad in it. Psalm 118:24

You may be wondering what middle school is going
to be like. Elementary school was pretty predictable:
get there in the morning, have the same teacher all day
long, and maybe even sit in the same seat. Morning
was math, reading, recess . . . well, you get the idea.
But what's it like at middle school?

Well, this handy, user-friendly guide is guaranteed
to clear up some of the mystery of what awaits you
beyond the walls of your new school.

START YOUR DAY

The best way to start your day is by spending a little time with the Lord. Maybe take five minutes to read your Bible, then take five minutes to pray. Just be honest and tell God everything that's on your mind.

Isaiah 45:6 says, "That they may know from the rising of the sun to its setting that there is none besides Me. I am the Lord, and there is no other." In other words, all day long we can know and rely on the Lord to be there for us.

Once you get to school, stop at your locker to make sure you've got all the books and supplies that you need for your morning classes.

Thinking inside the box: your locker

There are basically two kinds of lockers in the known world: the "supply your own lock" locker and the "lock is built-in" locker. If you supply your own lock, the combination will be printed on the back of the package. The combination for a built-in lock will be given to you on the first day of school.

Keep your combination in your wallet or purse—somewhere safe, but close by—so when you need it, it'll be right there. Don't share your combination with any of your friends. That's your combination and you'll need it to keep your locker secure and your stuff safe.

If you forget the combination of your built-in locker, just go to the office and someone there can give it to you again. No big deal. But just like a lot of things in middle school, after three or four days, your locker combination will become deeply ingrained in your memory.

One time I locked myself inside my locker.

You may have to share your locker with another student. Your locker partner may be your really close friend, or he may just be someone you've never met before. You don't need to be best friends with your locker-mate, but make sure you show him respect and don't take or mess with his stuff.

✹Bright Idea: Don't keep valuable stuff like CDs, jewelry, or money in your locker. Those things could be a little too tempting for some people to leave alone.

WHAT IS MY HOMEROOM?

Think of homeroom as the launching pad for
the rest of your day. There you may hear the day's
announcements, register your attendance, and take
care of school business.

Room 201? You can't get there from here.

Now you're off to morning classes. But first you have
to find them! When you think about finding your way
around your huge, confusing new middle school,
do you picture yourself drowning in a sea of kids
who all seem to know exactly where they're going?

Don't panic! First of all, you've got to believe you're not
the only person in the whole school who's feeling this
way. Look around you. There's a whole bunch of new
kids who—even though they're not admitting it out
loud—are just as nervous as you. Even the teachers
were new once!

One of the best ways to get over what the experts call "Middle School Gargantua-phobia" (or the fear of very large middle schools) is to take a little trip over to the place before the school year begins. Ask a friend or your brother or sister who has been there to show you around.

If you get your class schedule ahead of time, circle your classrooms on a map of the campus. That will get you familiar with the layout. Who knows? Maybe you'll be the one giving directions the first day.

Once school starts, don't be afraid to ask a teacher or an older student where something is. Everybody does that. It doesn't mean you're dumb. In fact, what's dumber than not asking directions and wandering in the halls for two or three hours?

SORTING OUT YOUR CLASSES

By now you realize that in middle school, you're going to have several classes and several teachers, and as a result, several seats throughout the day.

"Why do they do that?" you may ask. As you move up in grades, you will need more specialized classes in things like math, science, and history. So middle school teachers specialize in these various studies. For example, your history teacher may have majored in history in college. He probably knows absolutely tons about that subject. Just ask him. The same goes for your math teacher, science teacher, and so on. So you'll learn a ton of stuff in each class and be a total braniac when you're all done.

"How will I remember all that stuff?" you may cry. Here's how the normal middle schooler's brain operates.

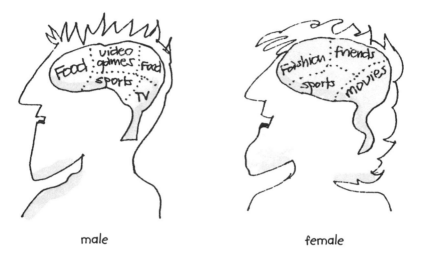

male

female

So as you can see, your brain is divided up into different parts so you can store all the stuff you learn throughout the day. And don't worry, even if you learn a whole lot in one day, you've still got loads of room in your brain for important stuff like friends and TV, music, and swimming lessons.

LUNCH

Ninety percent of all students polled indicate that lunch is their favorite subject in school. Just kidding, but it is a nice break from the heavy brain activity you've been into all morning. Plus it's a chance to see friends, catch up on the latest school news, and grab some nutrition.

I Love Lunch!

One thing you may notice pretty quickly is that most middle schools have more than one lunch period. That could mean you won't be eating with your friends.

If that happens, you have a few options:

1. Try to change your schedule so you can eat with some buddies. This could, however, mess up all your classes.

2. Make the best of it, and try to meet some new people.

3. Change your name to François, and tell everyone you're the new exchange student from France. Let them know that your nutritional needs require you to eat at a certain time of day (which, of course, is the time when your friends are eating).

Lunch is so much more than just a peanut butter sandwich and stale potato chips. It can be a rich dining experience where you enjoy delightful nutritious edibles along with scintillating conversation with your fellow students. In other words, it's a good social time.

If you're one of the lucky kids who gets to buy lunch in the cafeteria, study the cafeteria menu in advance. You can figure out which days you want to eat there, and which days you definitely *don't* want to eat there. Eddie and Todd have taken the liberty of translating their school menu for you. Now you'll know what the cooks really mean when they say "Chef's Choice".

Weekly Cafeteria Menu
with translation by Todd and Eddie

Tuna Surprise
  This means that it'll be
  a surprise if you find
  any tuna in it.

Take-Out Oven Pizza
  Yeah, they forgot to take it out of the oven in time!

Sloppy Joe's
  Just who is Joe anyway? And why is he so sloppy?
  Is it because these are just hamburgers with too
  much ketchup?

Chef's Choice
  This is just a nice way of saying leftovers.
  I call it "A Week-at-a-Glance" buffet. Forget what
  you had on Wednesday? Don't worry. It'll be back,
  repackaged for your enjoyment, on Friday.

AFTERNOON

The morning is behind you. You made it! Next is
another stop at your locker and then afternoon classes.
But don't think that your day is even close to finished.
You're in middle school now, so you have lots more
to do. You may even have activities after school
(like sports and stuff). Then it's time to tackle
your homework. Whew! You sure are busy!

But don't sweat it. Middle school can be a really
cool time for you—especially if you get involved
with fun things that weren't available to you before
(we'll talk about some of those things in the next
couple of chapters).

⬥ REALITY CHECK

Starting a new thing—any new thing—can be nerve-wracking and downright overwhelming. In fact, you may be scared stiff! But you know what? These feelings are completely natural. Like we said at the start of this book, change is hard and everybody gets nervous when things change.

Here's the thing. God cares all about what you're going through and what you're feeling right now! In fact, the Bible says that he knows every single hair on your head (think about that the next time you get a haircut)! Not only does God know when you're having trouble, but he cares about it, too. Tell him how you're feeling. Just say something like "Hi, God, I'm a little nervous about my first day," or "Dear Lord, I'm afraid nobody's going to like me. Will you go with me through this day?" Not only will God hear you, but he promises to stick by your side. In fact, in Hebrews 13:5 God says to you, "I will never leave you nor forsake you."

Here, we'll start a prayer and then you finish it
with your own words:

Dear Lord,
It's cool that you really do care about
me going to school. I know in my head that
you're with me, but I pray that you'll
help me feel it, too. And the things that
I really need help with now are:

You
Are
Here

Anna found out soon enough
that there were better ways
to choose her electives . . .

CHAPTER 2:

Electives

I will praise You, for I am fearfully
and wonderfully made. Psalm 139:14

One cool thing about some middle schools is you get
to choose some fun classes to take. These are called
electives. Electives are a great place to get started with
new interests. Are you the type who likes to paint or
make pottery? Are you a natural "ham" who loves to get
up in front of people? Or maybe you like knitting or
basket weaving.

Even though God's probably not going to show you what class to take in those ways, there are some things you can do to make a good decision.

How to make a good decision

1. Pray about it. Ask God to help you figure out what classes to choose.

2. Check out God's Word. The Bible can give you direction for any question in your life.

3. Figure out what you like. You've got natural talents and interests that God has given you. Here is your chance to develop them. Don't forget God wants to use your talents for his purposes.

4. Talk to other people. Your mom and dad and other older Christians know things that you don't. The book of Proverbs says that having lots of counselors will give you wisdom. In other words, asking others for advice will help you make good choices.

So now that you've got some ideas on how to make your choice, here's a list of elective classes some middle schoolers can choose.

Shop

Do you like to design and build things? Do you like working with wood or metal? Than you could look into a shop class. These are fun classes if you are a "hands-on" learner. Plus you usually end up with a cool project or two at the end of the semester. You may learn some drafting and design in here, too.

Home economics

It used to be that only girls would take home economics—you know, cooking, sewing, and household stuff. But guys should think about taking this class, too. A few years ago you could look forward to making a fried egg in the middle of a piece of toast. But nowadays the sky's the limit. Cakes, pies, pizzas, healthy breakfasts—it's all there. Hey guys, you could turn out to be some of the best cooks in the school! It's good for everyone to learn about healthy nutrition, balancing your checkbook, and taking care of a home.

Art

Are you an artsy person who likes to draw, paint, or sculpt? Then you definitely should be checking out an art class. Middle school art classes are cool because they start to focus on the specifics of art. Color, design, composition (where things go in the picture)—you'll be able to explore all these things and more. If you're one of the fortunate people who can express themselves through art (or want to be), you definitely should go for an art class.

Physical education

At some schools P.E., or physical education, is a requirement, but sometimes it's an elective. Either way, P.E. can be a really fun class. It gives you a much-needed break from all the brain activity you're doing all day and gives you a chance to run around! A P.E. class will give you a chance to try a lot of different sports like football, tennis, volleyball, basketball, lacrosse, and maybe even the two-man luge. If you're not very good at all of these, don't worry. You'll probably find two or three sports that you really like and are good at.

By the way, you may end up with a P.E. teacher like Coach Rorshauk. He was 63 pounds at birth and could bench-press 240 by the time he was three. He had two dreams for his future: either become a maximum security prison warden, or a seventh grade P.E. teacher. Well, the prison system won and guess who lost? Welcome to Camp Rorshauk.

Drop and give me 50!

FOREIGN LANGUAGES

Como estas? Parlez-vous Français? Wouldn't it be cool to be able to speak a foreign language? You could work as an interpreter or an international tour guide or even a spy. Learning languages is another great thing about middle school.

The two most common languages taught in middle school are Spanish and French, but your school may offer Italian or even Japanese. Learning a language is challenging, but the more you practice, the better you'll get. After you've been in class awhile, rent a movie in the language you're studying and see how much of it you can follow.

You could check to see if your church supports a missionary to a place that speaks the language you're learning. Get the missionary's address and write her a letter. She would love to hear from you and it'll be great practice for you.

You are here

Bright Idea: If you really want to make a great impression on your foreign language teacher, just learn these phrases and say them to him on the first day of class.

Buenos Dias.
Quiero decirle
cuanto anhelo su
clase excelente.
Estoy animado
a sentarme y
aprender
del mejor. Soy y
siempre sere tu
servidor humilde.

Spanish

(Translation: Good Day. I want to tell you how much I'm looking forward to your excellent class. I'm excited to sit and learn from the best. I am, and will always be, your humble servant.)

Hey, if you still can't figure out where your interests lie, take this official quiz.

Personality quiz
Answer the following questions—
either Yes, No, or No Way!

I like to build things like models, tree forts, and fences.
    Yes   **No**   **No Way**
Did you say yes to this one? You could check out a shop class. You could do either wood shop, metal shop, or drafting.

One of my favorite things to do is make up stories.
    Yes   **No**   **No Way**
Yes? You could try a class in creative writing. Check with the English teacher to see if your school has one.

I'm a natural-born entertainer.
    Yes   **No**   **No Way**
If you said yes, you should definitely look into a drama or voice class. Who knows? You may be a star.

I'm really into sports, big-time.
    Yes   **No**   **No Way**
Was that a yes? You'd have a blast in a P.E. class. Watch out for Coach Rorshauk though. Get ready for some serious push-ups.

I love drawing, painting, and creative stuff like that.
    Yes   **No**   **No Way**
You'll want to get into an art class and start creating as soon as you can. You'll love it!

 REALITY CHECK

God did a wonderful job of making you who you are. Your unique gifts, talents, and abilities are all part of God's design. Don't feel overwhelmed by all the choices and decisions you'll face in middle school. Instead, ask God to help you use these new opportunities to further develop your talents. God will help you to be all that he created you to be.

BOTTOM LINE

First Corinthians says that the followers of Jesus are like one body where everybody plays an important part. You fit in the body, too. What part do you play? It's up to you to discover your gifts and to develop them as much as you can. God will do the rest.

Take a moment and write down some of the dreams you have for your life. Ask God to partner with you in this exciting adventure.

Although attending a small middle school
had many advantages,
orchestra wasn't one of them . . .

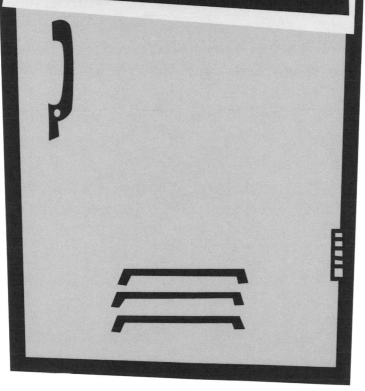

CHAPTER 3:

Extracurricular activities

I have come that they may have life, and that they may have it more abundantly. John 10:10

Just like in other parts of your life, you will get out of middle school what you put into it. You could just go to school, do the work and get through it, or you could really dive in and take advantage of all the cool opportunities that are now available to you. Extracurricular activities are the things that can make your middle school experience rich, fun, and rewarding. And they're one of the ways God may use to grow you up to be an awesome individual.

There are lots of benefits to getting involved in extracurricular activities:

1. It's a great way to meet some new friends.

2. As you participate in these things, you'll get better and better at them. And as you improve, you'll feel really good about yourself.

3. By starting some of these things now, you're going to be prepared for the next level of activity in high school.

4. The best thing about getting involved in one or more of these activities is you're going to have fun!

SPORTS

The first thing most kids think of when you say extracurricular activities is sports. Middle school is a great time to join a team, try a new sport, or improve the skills you already have.

Some popular sports in middle school are:
For Guys–Football, basketball, soccer, wrestling, baseball, and track.
For Girls–Volleyball, soccer, basketball, softball, cheerleading, and track.

Most of these sports practice after school and have a grade requirement in order to participate. So make sure you're also doing your schoolwork and keeping your grades up, or you'll be removed from the team.

At the beginning of the school year, you'll get information on how and when to sign up for a particular sport. There may be a fee to cover uniforms and referees, so make sure you know what that is. And don't miss the sign-up deadline!

Todd Reebok has been involved in pretty much every sport there is and he's usually first-team. So what's his secret? Here are some of his tryout and sporting hints to help you shine.

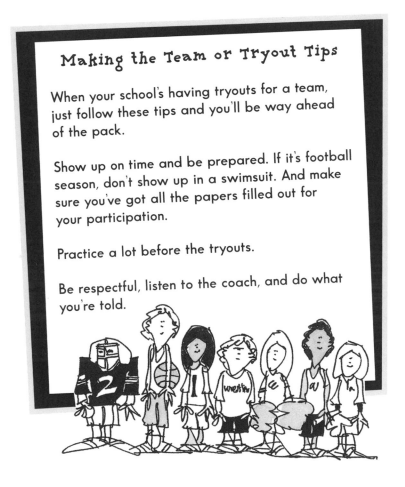

Making the Team or Tryout Tips

When your school's having tryouts for a team, just follow these tips and you'll be way ahead of the pack.

Show up on time and be prepared. If it's football season, don't show up in a swimsuit. And make sure you've got all the papers filled out for your participation.

Practice a lot before the tryouts.

Be respectful, listen to the coach, and do what you're told.

Try not to be disappointed if the coach wants you for a different position than you tried out for. He sees the whole picture and may have a different plan in mind.

If you don't get picked at all, that feels pretty bad. It's OK to feel sad, bad, disappointed, or even angry. But don't let those feelings hang on too long. Tell God what you're feeling. Be honest. And don't give up! Find out what you can work on for next time and try again. You'll be glad you did.

I don't understand this!

Be a good sport

Now that you've made the team, good sportsmanship is really important. If you've given your life to Jesus, sports can be a great place to show how God's working in you. Don't argue, get mad, throw things, or have tantrums. God wants us to be different: not selfish, spoiled, or obnoxious. Does that mean we don't play hard, or don't care if we win or lose? Of course not. Nobody likes to win as much as I do. But when we remember that God's our ultimate coach, it helps keep things in perspective.

Listen to the coach.

Coach is the head honcho. He really does know what he's doing. Respect him and listen to what he's saying. Don't talk or mess around when he's talking. Whenever I have a question or a suggestion, I wait for a good time and then I just ask Coach. Remember, Christians should respect the leaders God puts over us.

Be teachable.

Proverbs 10:8 and 13:18 say how important it is to be teachable and able to receive instruction. Listen to suggestions your coach makes to help you improve. Listen to him, then try it the way he says. That's the best way to learn and grow as an athlete—and as a person. Trust me on this.

Try your hardest.
You may feel like you're not very good at a particular sport. Don't let that bother you. Hey! Even I wasn't very good at stuff once! But if you listen to the coach and do your best, you'll get better. A lot better. And especially if you make sure you . . .

Practice. Practice. Practice.
Practice all you can. At school, at home, at . . . practice. The more you do it, the better you'll get. Find a buddy or teammate to practice with. Rent some videos that show you how to play the game or check out some books from the library. There may be some clinics or sports camps going on in your community. Look at me. I practice. I go to camps. I'm cool. I'm the best athlete around. I'm fast. I'm coordinated, and most of all, I'm totally humble.

MUSIC

There are lots of opportunities to get involved in music in your new school. Most middle schools have a band or orchestra as well as a choir. This may be a great time for you to learn an instrument. You could try the piano, the guitar, or even the trombone. Find out who the music teacher is and talk to her about opportunities in that field.

You may have to audition for a spot, but don't let that make you nervous. Just practice like crazy, do your best, and remember that the teacher wants you to do well even more than you do.

DRAMA

Have you always dreamed of being a star? Middle school may just be your chance to do it. Many schools do one or two drama productions a year. If you're interested, go talk to the director of the show or the drama teacher. Find out when the auditions will be and what you'll need to do for them.

The rehearsals will probably be after school, so make sure your schedule and your homework fit in with that. Don't worry if you love the theatre but can't imagine getting up in front of all those people. There are always lots of behind-the-scenes jobs for you to do. Props, lights, sound, and costumes are fun and may just fit your talents and abilities.

Kacey Joiner is an eighth grader who's involved in almost everything. She's been a natural "ham" since she was about two years old and tries out for every show that comes along. She has agreed to give us some of her tips for getting ahead in the theatre.

Kacey Tells You the Secret of Becoming a Star
(or how to give a great audition)

These tips have always helped me in my auditions. Maybe you caught me last year as Marion in *The Music Man* or the year before as Wendy in *Peter Pan*. The year before that I was the third townswoman in . . . well, never mind. If you blinked, you missed me.

But here are some sure-fire audition tips that'll really help you on the road to success:
Be prepared before you get to the audition. If scripts are available before the tryout date, check one out ahead of time and see which part may be right for you. Find all the scenes that your character is in and read them a few times. Usually I don't memorize the scenes, but I just get really familiar with them. That way, I'm confident when I audition.

If it's a musical and the director wants you to sing, come with a song you know. This should be memorized. One time I sang "Tomorrow" from Annie. I forgot the words half way through so I just kept singing "Tomorrow, Tomorrow, Tomorrow" for about seven minutes. Mr. Barker (the drama teacher) finally cut me off. You should also bring the song's piano sheet music for the audition accompanist.

My aunt plays the piano so I usually practice with her a few times before the audition. She always tells me to stand up straight.

When it's your turn to go, walk in, smile, and listen to the director's instructions. He may want you to audition alone or you may be in a small group of actors. Take a deep breath before you start, that always helps me relax. When you start reading try not to be "glued" to the script. Look up and make eye contact with the other actors. It makes the scene more real. Don't worry if you miss a word or make a mistake. The important thing is that the character and your personality come through. Most of all, have a good time.

Remember, this isn't brain surgery. Drama should be fun, so have a blast.

SPEECH

This activity teaches you to write and present speeches in front of an audience. Even stand-up comedy is a form of speech. Lots of times there are competitions with other schools in this field. Those can be really fun.

DEBATE TEAM

Do you like to argue? Do you always have to be right? Debating may be just for you. You get to research, write, and argue your case with other students. If you want to be a lawyer or politician, debating is for you.

VIDEO PRODUCTION

Make your own mini-movies, TV productions, commercials, animation, or sci-fi thrillers. You get to write, produce, and direct! Be creative. Get a group of friends to write and act in the video. Then edit it, and add special effects and graphics. You'll have a blast.

RADIO PRODUCTION

If you like music, try radio production. Be an on-air personality and play cool CDs. Or work behind the scenes as an engineer or producer. You may end up being broadcast through the whole school.

✳Bright Idea: If an activity interests you, but there's no program for it, why not start one? Find an interested adult to help organize it.
Who knows? You may start something really exciting.

STUDENT GOVERNMENT

Posters, rallies, speeches, campaigns! Does all that sound fun to you? Then you should look into running for a student office. You can run for student council, or try a leadership position like president, vice president, treasurer, or secretary.

STUDENT COUNCIL

A lot of schools have the kids elect other kids to represent them at council meetings just like we elect our representatives to Congress. Then rather than going to the meetings themselves, their elected representatives go and submit ideas.

For example, if you think a cookie machine would be a nice addition to the courtyard, you tell your student council reps and they bring it up at the meeting. Or you could be the council member. It's fun and a great way to get involved in the politics around the school. Find out which teacher is in charge of all of this political stuff for your school and let her know you're interested. She'll tell you what to do.

Student council can be a great experience and a chance to work with other kids to make a positive difference in your school. Now you may be asking yourself, "Should I consider running for class officer?" Oliver Flavinoid has run for almost everything so turn the page for his simple guide to middle school politics.

The Inside World of
Middle School Politics
by Oliver Flavinoid

Sit back and relax and I'll let you in on some of the secrets of school politics. I ought to know them, I've run for every office there is.

President

Obviously this is a very responsible job and probably takes the most time. The president usually runs all the council meetings which means you'll need to be familiar with the rules of order and be a courteous and good leader. The class president may represent the school at outside functions with parents and teachers so make sure your comfortable with that. Knowing how to make small talk in social situations is a big plus. But really, being president is tons of fun.

Vice President

The vice president, or VP as we call her, serves whenever the president is gone or sick. Last year, when the president was sick with the flu, Jamie Steinbrenner ran the meeting. She almost passed a "Guys Serve the Girls Day" but Coach Rorshauk, our faculty sponsor, squashed that idea.

Anyway, being VP is cool because you're right up there helping make important decisions without the pressure of being the one totally in charge.

Secretary

The secretary is in charge of keeping the minutes of all the meetings. That means you take notes on who said what and why and when. Then you type them up later.

If you're a good listener and a fast writer with clear handwriting, you'd probably make a good secretary. Two years ago Stephanie Arbuckle was secretary. Once she wrote her notes so fast that instead of getting "new basketball hoops for the gym" we almost got "blue socket loops for the gum." She wasn't re-elected.

Treasurer

Just because you're the treasurer doesn't mean you have to love money. But you'd better be organized with it! Sometimes you'll be in charge of collecting the cash for a fundraiser or a social. The treasurer is also in charge of paying all the bills for the expenses completely and on time. If you're pretty organized, especially in finances, then treasurer is for you.

Mr.
President

⚓ REALITY CHECK

Extracurricular activities are the things that make middle school fun, exciting, and challenging. And you know what? God has some interesting stuff planned for you! When Jesus was on earth, he said that he had come to give us life, and life more abundantly. His plan isn't for us just to survive through life—but to succeed, grow, and experience all he has for us. He even wants us to have fun! It may be a little intimidating to try out for a team or play, but think of it this way—you've got nothing to lose!

It may be hard, but the rewards are so cool that it's definitely worth it. You could end up being an awesome soccer forward, second baseman, or the next star of the school play. Go for it! You'll be glad you did.

BOTTOM LINE

The word that Jesus used when he was talking about abundant life was the Greek word "perissos" (pronounced per-ee-SOSS) and it means superabundance, overflowing, excessive, surplus, more than enough. When Jesus gives us life, it's so much deeper and richer and fuller than we can even imagine. That's the kind of Lord he is. A superabundant one!

Now that you know EVERYTHING about extracurricular stuff at school, write about what YOU may go for.

Here's what sports I may try out for . . .

Here's what I think about these activities . . .

	sounds fun	maybe	not if you paid me
drama			
speech			
chess club			
debate			
radio			

I'm thinking of running for student government. Here are my campaign slogans . . .

Having organized his desk, notebook,
file cards, computer, lamp, paper,
pencils, and eraser, Chad couldn't
remember what class he was studying for!

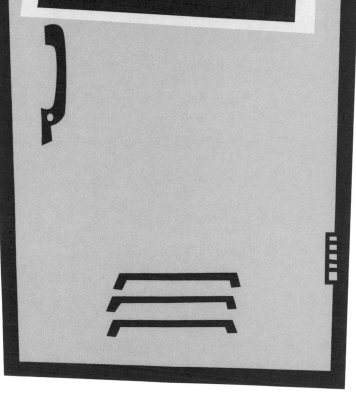

CHAPTER 4:

What you need to succeed

You were faithful over a few things, I will make you ruler over many things. Matthew 25:21

SCHOOL MATERIALS

As you get ready to start middle school you should probably think about your school supplies. You don't have to spend a lot of money, but there are some things you're going to need when you get there. Your school may even send you a list of supplies you're going to need.

One thing you're going to need is a notebook or binder. This is going to be your "home base" where you'll keep papers and assignments from all your classes. Make sure you keep your notebook organized. It'll make your life a lot easier. Get some page dividers, too. These go into your binder and separate your classes. They've got little tabs so you can find stuff quickly.

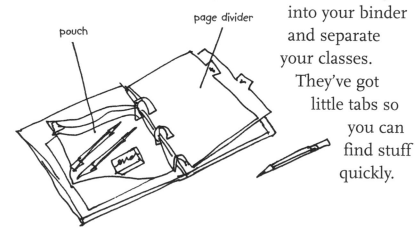

page divider

pouch

Inside the front part of your notebook you'll want to have a little plastic pouch. These have three rings so they can clip right inside your binder. You can keep your pencils (keep 2 or 3 sharpened), pens (black or blue ink), glue stick, erasers, paper clips, and other stuff in there.

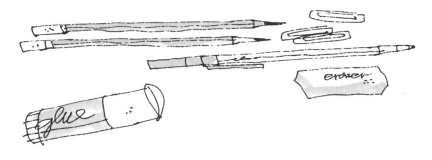

Always keep a good supply of paper in your notebook so you don't run out at an important time. Usually you'll want 8 1/2" by 11" lined paper with three holes and a margin. Just for fun, keep track of the times when someone who hasn't read this book says, "Can I borrow a piece of paper? I forgot mine."

paper

MORE SUPPLIES FOR MATH

Most middle schools require you to buy a calculator to use during your math classes. You can get a good calculator for between $10 and $15 and you'll be glad you have it. Your school can give you an idea of where to get one. If you're in advanced math you may have to get a graphing calculator and those can run around a hundred bucks.

calculator

You're also going to need a ruler to use during your math classes. The best kind to get are made of wood with a metal edge and three holes so it can fit into your notebook.

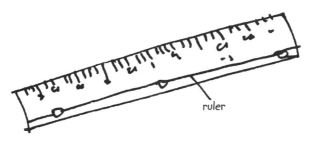

ruler

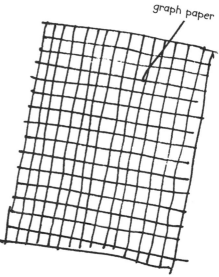

graph paper

Another thing you're going to need for most of your math classes is a pad of graph paper. You're going to need this for doing graphs and charts.

BACKPACK WISDOM

For about the last fifteen years, kids have been taking backpacks to school. That's because they're really convenient. You can stick your books, papers, projects, and lunch inside and off you go. But there are some drawbacks to backpacks. Some young people start to develop back and shoulder problems because their backpacks are too heavy.

Here are some backpack guidelines that'll save some wear and tear on your body:

Lighten up!
Your backpack should weigh between 10 and 15% of your weight. For example, if you weigh 100 pounds, your backpack should weigh around 10 to 15 pounds. Clean out papers weekly and only take the books home that you'll need for that night. Keep your extra books in your locker.

Go wide

Backpacks with wider straps are better for you because they distribute the weight more evenly. So try to get one that has wide straps. When you pick up your backpack, it's really easy to just put one strap over your shoulder, but it's a lot better for you to wear both straps evenly.

Balance things out

When you're filling your backpack, put the heaviest items closest to your back. That way you don't have to strain to counterbalance them. Heavier things like big books and your binder should go in first. Paperbacks and your lunch go in after that.

100 pounds   10 – 15 pounds

GET ORGANIZED

One of the most important things you can learn in middle school is how to be organized. And the sooner you get organized, the better you'll do in your classes. Your binder should be divided into different sections to deal with each class. When you get to class, pull out your binder and get to the section that deals with that subject. Get a clean sheet of paper and jot down the important stuff the teacher says—especially things like an upcoming test and what will be on it.

Also, write down your homework assignments and when they're due. That way, you won't be totally clueless about what you're supposed to do when you get home.

Try to keep up with the work from the very beginning. It's easier than trying to catch up after you've gotten behind. And if you get confused, lost, or totally behind, just ask a friend or the teacher for some help.

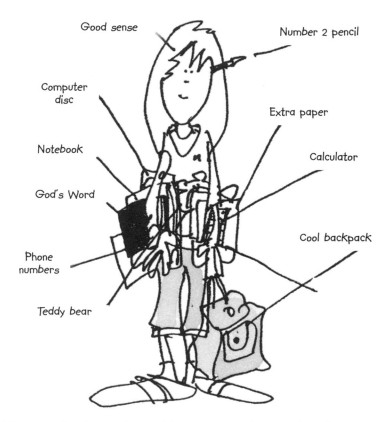

Good sense

Number 2 pencil

Computer disc

Extra paper

Notebook

Calculator

God's Word

Phone numbers

Cool backpack

Teddy bear

The totally-together middle schooler

AND NOW FOR THE POPULAR MID-BOOK FEATURE: ASK FLAV!

Today Oliver Flavinoid, or Flav as he's known at school, is answering questions about common challenges to learning.

Ask Flav!

Question:
What if I'm really trying, but I just can't understand the material?

Answer:
First of all, don't feel bad. Nobody can be great in every class. I bet Albert Einstein was awful in ceramics! You've got several options. One option is to talk to your teachers. They really are there to help you. Often teachers come in early or stay after school to help kids individually. So if you're having trouble in a subject, just talk to your teacher. Asking for help is one of the smartest things you can do.

If you're still having trouble, get some help at home. Ask your parents to check your work and help you with it. Or you could even get a tutor to help you out. Often a high school or college student who actually understands the stuff can work with you.

But the important thing is that you don't give up. You really can do it if you get some help.

More Ask Flav!

Question:
I really have trouble staying tuned-in during class. What should I do?

Answer:
Make sure you're getting enough sleep every night. Sometimes when we're tired, we have trouble staying tuned in.

Try taking notes on what the teacher's talking about. I've found that the action of writing sometimes will keep me focused and will even help me remember the material.

Watch your sugar intake throughout the day. Is there a certain time of day when it's hard to concentrate? It may be right after lunch or late in the afternoon. Be careful not to eat too many sweets during the day. They could be affecting your concentration and making you sleepy.

More Ask Flav!

Question:
I can't see the board or even the teacher very well.

Answer:
You may need glasses or contacts. When was the last time you had your eyes checked? Ask your mom or dad. Glasses are kind of hip right now. Maybe your glasses will even make a fashion statement like mine do. Sometimes just being moved to the front of the class can help you see better, too.

Question:
What if I understand the stuff, but I don't care and don't do the work so my grades are really bad.

Answer:
You're not alone. There are a lot of really smart kids out there who just aren't trying so their grades are lousy. First, you've got to ask yourself why this is happening. It could be that the material is too easy and you're bored with it. Maybe you should get into a more advanced level class.

Is something bothering you and you can't seem to figure a way out of it? Is there something wrong at home? Are you having problems with friends or maybe feeling like you've got no friends?

Stress like that can affect your ability to focus on schoolwork. Schoolwork seems kind of meaningless when your parents are divorcing or you feel like you've lost all your friends. If something like that is going on, you really need to talk with someone you trust. Try your youth pastor, teacher, or counselor.

And this would definitely be a time to pray. Just tell God what's going on. You don't have to use special words or phrases. Just say something like, "God, could you help me out of this? Give me someone to talk to and please help me with _____. OK? Thanks. Talk to you later. Amen."

God hears you and wants to help. He really does. Just ask him.

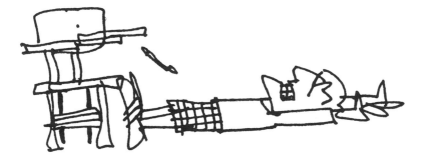

More Ask Flav!

Question:
As a Christian, how do I handle stuff in class I don't agree with?

Answer:
That's a great question. For example, what if your science teacher starts talking about the theory of evolution, or your English teacher brings up some weird spiritual stuff like reincarnation or something? How should you respond? You could:

1. Stand up and shout "No, no, no! You can't say that! We Christians think that's a bunch of hogwash and you're evil for saying it!"

2. Just go along with their ideas and don't say anything.

3. Quietly stew in the back row.

4. Ask God how he wants you to respond.

If you chose 4, you're on the right track. Ask God how to respond. It could be different every time. Sometimes you're not to say anything. Other times he'll want you to talk to the teacher later. At that point, respectfully tell the teacher that you don't agree with her position on the topic.

Don't argue or be self-righteous, but try speaking the truth in love (Ephesians 4:15). You could even study the topic from a Biblical standpoint. Check out some Christian books on the subject.

By the way, this whole "speaking the truth in love" thing goes for when you talk to your friends about stuff, too. Think about it. Which would you rather respond to: someone telling you that you're a dumb, evil sinner, or someone who comes alongside of you and kindly shares about the love of God?

DO YOUR HOMEWORK

Now that you're in middle school, you'll have more homework than you've ever had before. That's because you're learning more and are smarter than you were before. Trust me, it's a good trade-off. Here's another article from Flav with some smart study advice.

Studying: How I Do It.
by Oliver "Flav" Flavinoid

Hi there. Oliver Flavinoid here, letting you in on some of the ways really smart kids like me get their homework done, have time to have fun, and still get all A's . . . almost.

First of all you want to have a set time to study. Do you like to do it right away, when you get home? I usually do that. But some of my friends, like Todd, get home and need some time to unwind first. He has a snack, or maybe shoots some baskets, then he's ready to work. Eddie . . . well, Eddie's still working on some homework from 1998.

A little trick I use is to do my hardest homework first—when I'm fresh. Then I do the easier or fun stuff. For example, I do my math assignments first. They're the hardest for me.

Then when I'm done with the hard stuff, I do history and science. In my English class, we have to make a poster about a famous person we've been studying. I'll do that last because it's the easiest.

I usually do my homework at my desk. I've got a computer there and everything's within my reach. My sister likes to lie on the floor and work there. It doesn't really matter where you are as long as you've got good light where you're working. It's supposed to be good to work at the same place everyday. It's like your brain says "Oh, I'm at the desk, so it must be homework time."

I don't take any phone calls while I'm doing homework. It kind of breaks my momentum. Then when I take a break, I call the person back. Come to think of it, nobody ever calls me so that hasn't been a problem. Hmmm.

Speaking of breaks, it's important to take a study break once in a while, just to give your brain a breather. Get up, get something to eat, pet the dog, bug your sister—anything to get the blood moving.

Well, that's about it from here. This is Oliver Flavinoid saying so long and happy studying.

Mom, anybody call for me?

Comfortable chair

Lamp

Computer

Pencils

REALITY CHECK

What's the big deal about being organized or having all the right supplies? For one thing, being organized really does make your life easier. If you spend time every day looking for lost stuff, or if you can't ever remember the assignment you're supposed to be working on, you may need to get it together in this area.

But do what works for you. Make up your own system. When you do your homework or where you drop your books may not seem all that important, but God really does watch what we do with the small things in our lives. Jesus said that when we're faithful with the little things, then the Father knows he can trust us with bigger things.

It kind of makes sense doesn't it? If we're responsible with the small stuff, it shows we can handle more important assignments. Try it. God's watching. And he wants to trust you with more.

BOTTOM LINE

Now what are some small things you can do right now to show the Lord that your faithfulness is growing?

I'm ready to get organized. Here are some organizing tips I want to try . . .

It's smart to do the most difficult homework first.
Here's how I rank my homework:

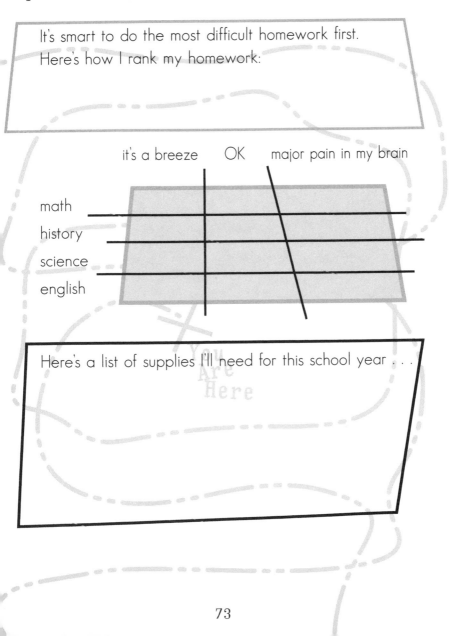

it's a breeze   OK   major pain in my brain

math

history

science

english

Here's a list of supplies I'll need for this school year . . .

Middle school fact #347: Nobody actually
dances at middle school dances.

CHAPTER 5:

Your social life

"For I know the thoughts that I think toward you," says the Lord, "thoughts of peace and not of evil, to give you a future and a hope." Jeremiah 29:11

EVERYBODY FEELS THAT WAY

Probably the biggest challenge as you go into middle school isn't the schoolwork or the new schedule. It isn't gym class or even your locker. The biggest challenge is surviving socially. What does that mean? It means things like making friends, getting involved, and generally feeling like you belong . . . and that you matter.

Things are different in middle school. Little groups or even cliques develop. Kids that were your friends before, now act like they don't know you. And kids that used to be nice may turn mean. You may be feeling insecure or unpopular. You are about to be let in on the most guarded secret in the entire middle school universe. Are you ready? Maybe you'd better sit down.

Here it is . . . Are you sure you can handle this?

Everybody feels that way.
Yup. You got it right. I repeat:
Everybody feels that way.

Last semester Oliver (Flav) Flavinoid did a research paper on how people respond to moving into a new situation, for example, going from elementary to middle school.

His findings are astounding. Read the excerpt from his report on the next pages . . .

Dealing with Change
(and I don't mean quarters, nickels, and dimes)

After spending some time in the middle school atmosphere, I've developed a keen understanding of the inner-workings of the typical middle school student. As youngsters make the transition from elementary to middle school, there are a number of things that I have observed taking place.

First, and foremost, I've observed a marked conversion of relational personnel. Sorry, in English this means kids change friends. You may have been really close to someone for years, but now all of a sudden, you aren't even friends anymore. Don't be surprised if that happens to you. There are a couple of reasons for this phenomenon.

One reason could be that you and your old friends have different classes, schedules, and even lunch periods. So you just don't see them very much. When you don't see people, it's hard to build a friendship.

Another reason is you may start developing different interests. You may be into basketball and snowboarding while your old friends may be heading towards music, art, and theatre. Hey, there's nothing wrong with that. It just means you all may have to work a little harder at doing stuff together. Go to their concerts or plays and offer to teach them how to snowboard.

The good news is these changes give you a chance to meet some new people. If it's hard for you to talk to people you don't know, start with someone who's in one of your classes. That'll give you something to talk about. Just say something like "Wow, who would've guessed the War of 1812 actually was in 1812!" or "How about them quadratic formulas?" That'll get the conversational ball rolling. It always works for me.

WITH FRIENDS LIKE THESE...

How can one thing be the best thing about middle school and also the hardest? No, we're not talking about Algebra. We're talking about people. We're talking about friends.

Some kids will breeze into middle school with a good, large set of friends who will be great fun and support the whole time. But a lot of kids may find that making and keeping friends is a challenge.

Some of the best ways to make friends are to show kindness, to reach out, and to listen to people. Those are the kinds of things people really appreciate.

On the other hand, there are ways to drive friends away. Read this top ten list of things to avoid in your friendships.

Top 10 Ways to Ruin a Friendship

10. Lie to your friend.

9. When school pictures come out, ask to borrow your friend's, then draw mustaches on all of them. Don't forget the wallet-sized.

8. Talk behind your friend's back.

7. If your friend is running for student government, stuff the ballot box . . . for his opponent.

6. Make fun of your friend's weaknesses.

5. When you're upset with your friend, don't talk to him about it, instead talk to everybody else.

4. Right as your friend's big soccer game is about to start, tie his shoelaces together.

3. Borrow things and forget to give them back.

2. When your friend is asleep, give him a haircut.

And the number 1 best way to ruin a friendship:

1. Forget the Golden Rule and just treat your friend like you'd never want him to treat you.

THE KEY TO MAKING (AND KEEPING) GOOD FRIENDS

What do you look for in a friend? Often, we make friends with someone who is interested in the same things we are. Or we like someone who has the same sense of humor or is our sports teammate. But if you think about it, things like loyalty, truthfulness, and honesty would be good things to look for, too. Take a minute and jot down some of the things you feel make for a good friend.

Now, think about yourself. These are good qualities that you should want to bring to any friendship. Ask God to help you be a good, honest, and true friend.

ODD MAN OUT

Have you ever thought about making an effort to reach out to some kids who may not have many friends themselves? What do you think would happen?

You could find a friend who's a really cool individual. When we judge people by how they look or what they do or don't do, we miss out on who they really are. You may think someone's really snobby because she won't talk to anyone. In reality, she could just be really shy.

Or you may see some kid who hangs out by himself and seems to be a geek. But actually, he's a great guy who's creative, clever, and funny. It's just that no one ever gets to see it. You may be the first!

God will help you and bless you as you go beyond yourself to initiate a friendship with a kid who's struggling. God loves that kid as much as he loves you. And he may just want to use *you* to let that kid know it.

By the way, if you're feeling like "that kid"—the one who nobody knows or cares about—remember that God doesn't make mistakes. He made you just the way you are. He loves you and wants the best for you. Read Psalm 139:1-18. This psalm describes how God feels about you!

PEER PRESSURE

Peer pressure. You hear that phrase all the time, but what does it mean? It's pressure from your peers—people your own age—to do what they do. Sometimes the pressure is to do stuff that you may not want to do.

There are some things you can do to handle this peer pressure deal.

BEING YOURSELF

Making right choices in the midst of peer pressure
1. Remember who you are—and *whose* you are. You're not just any kid. You're a child of the King. Remember those movies about the prince (or princess) who lived in the castle and all the food and clothes and kingship belonged to him? You've got to realize you're that kid!

Check out Galatians 4:4-7. We've been adopted into God's royal family! And if you belong to the One who created the sun, the moon, the galaxies, the world, Aunt Edna, and your dog, then what do you care if some guy doesn't think you're cool because you won't go smoke with him?

2. Another important thing to remember is that you should hang out with people who are good for you. You know what that means. Proverbs 12:26 says that you should choose your friends carefully because friends have the ability to lead us into trouble or keep us out of it! Spend time with kids that make you better.

3. Look at the big picture. Before you do something that you're not sure about, ask yourself these questions: How is this going to affect me or my parents? Is this something I'd like to appear in the paper tomorrow morning?

Think about the effects of what you're about to do. Is this worth it?

It would be really nice if you could go through life without ever having to face this kind of temptation. But since this is the real world, at some point you'll face the temptation to do something dumb.

✳Bright Idea: Did you know even Jesus was tempted? Look at what happened in Matthew 4:1-11. The enemy tried to get Jesus to shortcut what God had planned for him.

The smartest way to deal with temptation is to be prepared. Think ahead of time how you'll respond when something comes up. What will you say? What will you do?

Here. Try it for yourself. Here are a few scenarios of some things that could happen. How will you respond? Be creative with your ideas. Write down your plan on a piece of paper.

1. You're at the school social and a friend wants you to sneak out to smoke. What will you do?

2. You go over to somebody's house when her parents aren't there and she offers you a beer. What will you do?

3. A guy you're trying to impress asks you to let him copy your answers for a big test next period. What will you do?

4. At the drug store, one of your friends tells you to stick some candy bars in your shirt and walk out without paying. She says she does it all the time and never gets caught. What will you do?

5. A friend comes up with some pills he brought from home and tells you they give you tons more energy. You've got a busy day ahead and could use a boost, but . . . What will you do?

Nobody's faced more peer pressure than Eddie. You would too if you'd spent six years in middle school. You know, he looks pretty bad on the outside, but he actually has some good ideas for handling this peer pressure thing. Here's how he answers when his so-called friends try to get him to do stuff he doesn't agree with.

Eddie Piel's Guide
to withstanding Peer Pressure

Hey, I've been doing this awhile now so nobody messes with me anymore. But if they did, here's what I'd say:

If someone offers me a smoke
I say: No thanks, I can get the same effect by sucking on the exhaust pipe of my Aunt Clara's Oldsmobile.

If someone tries to get me to drink
I say: That sounds like fun: pouring alcohol down my throat, acting really stupid in front of people, then throwing up for two hours on the front lawn. All in all, a great night!

If someone wants to cheat off my paper
I say: Hmmm. No one's ever asked to copy my paper. But if someone did I'd say, "Oh, right, I'm going to risk both our grades by letting you cheat off me. Hey, next time I'll help you study for the test and you may actually learn something as well as ace the thing. OK?"

If someone wants me to steal from a store
I say: Oh, yeah. Like I want to end up on *America's Most Wanted* just because you were too cheap to pay for a pack of gum.

DEALING WITH A BULLY

What a drag. For some reason, you've become the target for a bigger or older kid (boy or girl) whose entire purpose in life is to make you miserable. He may be saying really mean things to you, or he may actually be pushing or hitting you.

Bullies have this way of making you feel scared or humiliated. After all, that's their goal. Bullies may even make you dread going to school each day. Here are some options for dealing with these people:

1. Daydream and do nothing. Picture your school without this obnoxious dweeb. (This usually doesn't help.)

2. Revenge. Bad idea. Yeah, it feels right, but this always leads to bad consequences.

3. Ignore him completely so it's no fun for him anymore. If he doesn't get a reaction from you, he'll usually lose interest.

4. Start to hang out in a group if you can. It's a rare bully who'll bother someone who's in a group. Talk to a friend about this so he's aware of it and can stick by you.

5. Try using some humor. Agree with the bully. "Yeah, you're right, I'm a loser. Why I'm so skinny, when I turn sideways and stick my tongue out, I look like a zipper! I've got to run around in the shower just to get wet! Hey this was fun, but I gotta' go, see ya!" (Then leave.)

6. If the bullying persists, try this: When he starts to harass you, just say firmly, "Leave me alone! Stop doing this!" Don't be angry or scared. Usually bullies don't get confronted like that. It kind of turns the tables and they don't know what to do. Most of the time, they'll stop bugging you.

The one thing that makes the most sense to do is pray. Ask God for wisdom and strength to deal with this guy. Pray for protection and that God will take care of the whole situation.

If things start to get really scary or if the situation is making your life totally miserable, you'll need to tell someone about it. Most schools have policies about bullying and the school authorities will step in. A lot of bullies will threaten, "If you tell anyone about this you're toast!" That's scary, but don't let that stop you. You're not trapped. You can get out of this.

WEAPONS AND THREATS

OK. Let's say one of your friends comes up and tells you he's so mad at someone, he's coming back to school tomorrow with a gun to blow him away. What do you do? Yipes!

The best thing you can do is tell a teacher, counselor, or even your mom or dad. Your telling someone may save a lot of grief. You could even save a life. Take it seriously.

✳**Bright Idea:** Middle school is for everybody. You've got the right to feel safe and hassle-free while you're there.

REALITY CHECK

You may end up having an awesome and fun experience in middle school, or this time in your life may be difficult. You may ask, "Why does God let me go through these tough times? Why can't I seem to do anything right? Why does God allow this bully to pick on me? Why can't middle school be fun?!?"

Does the fact that you're having a rough time mean that God doesn't care about you? Nope. God's highest priority for us is to be in relationship with him. Knowing him closely is more important than being rich, smart, popular, or even hassle-free. When we're hurt or lonely or scared, those seem to be the times when we'll come to God the most.

So if middle school is a bit of a challenge, remember that God's using all this hard stuff to get you closer to him. The best place you can ever be is close to your Creator.

BOTTOM LINE

Does this mean you've got to be really happy when someone's picking on you or you get lousy grades? Not at all. Those things are hard. Really hard. And as we've mentioned before, it's OK—in fact recommended—to do whatever you can to make things right. But in the meantime, realize that God's working overtime to get you to know him better. So trust him.

Whoa! There are a lot of things to think about when you're starting middle school! Classes, homework, friends, sports, acting, music, and even what to order in the cafeteria are all on your mind. But you know what? This is the beginning of a wonderful adventure called growing up.

No matter what you go through, God's got the whole thing under control. Just let him know what's going on in every part of your life—the good and the bad. He's always there. Going to middle school is just a part of the wonderful creative process that God's using to make you the kid (and grown-up) he's designed you to be. So go for it and enjoy this exciting time in your life.

Cool books for preteens!

SURVIVING
MIDDLE SCHOOL
written by
Sandy Silverthorne
0-7847-1433-9

SURVIVING
When You're
HOME ALONE
written by
Sandy Silverthorne
0-7847-1434-7

SURVIVING
ZITS
written by
Sandy Silverthorne
0-7847-1435-5

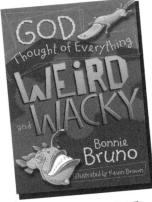

GOD THOUGHT OF
EVERYTHING
WEIRD & WACKY
written by
Bonnie Bruno
0-7847-1447-9

GOD THOUGHT OF
EVERYTHING
STRANGE & SLIMY
written by
Bonnie Bruno
0-7847-1448-7